A Dictionary of Mnemonics

A Dictionary
of Mnemonics

Eyre Methuen · London

First published 1972
by Eyre Methuen Limited
11 New Fetter Lane, London, EC4
© 1972 Eyre Methuen Limited
Printed in Great Britain
by Butler & Tanner Ltd
Frome and London
SBN 413 29430 7 hardback
SBN 413 28780 7 paperback

Contents

Publisher's Note

This is the first dictionary of its kind, and the memory-aids it gives will work on their own without the often elaborate systems required by other collections.

Times are bad for the memory-aid. Mnemonics were used in ancient Greece, but today their enemies say that learning from them is like learning about sex from dirty jokes; certainly teachers today mark creative thought higher than mere factual knowledge. If one has a memory, then all well and good. But many of the replies to our advertisements inviting material came from people who need help, in or out of the classroom, and who told us so.

We found the entries hard to select. One man's mnemonic can be another man's second good reason for forgetting something — the first of course being that he doesn't need to know it. How many people would use those fearsome anatomy mnemonics given to medics? Or a remembering-device that is entirely personal in form and application (we found many such)? Or the traditional classroom jingles which often tell only half the story, and often wrongly at that?

In the end we made a short selection of widely useful mnemonics, intelligible, at times elegant, and with somewhere a 'click' to them. We look forward to a second edition enlarged to include the mnemonic you convince us we should have put in. As with this edition, a free copy will be posted to the first sender of each entry printed.

Acknowledgements

The publishers have exercised all care in tracing and obtaining permission for the quotation of mnemonics as entries in the Dictionary. They regret if, in spite of this care, there has been any unintentional infringement of copyright, and meanwhile gratefully acknowledge the following (numbers refer to page and order on page) :

Dr D. M. Walker, University of Sydney	13a
Mr B. R. Bligh, Hampton Hill, Middx	13b
Mr P. V. Taberner, Southampton, Hants	13c
Dr R. W. Munn, Lasswade, Midlothian	14a
Mr A. English, Maida Vale, London, W.9	14b
Mr David C. Sutherland, University of Dundee	15
Mr Martin D. Pringle, Edinburgh	16
Mrs Janet Kershaw, East Didsbury, Manchester	17a
Mrs Mary Hargreaves, Grange-O-Sands, Lancs	17b, 21b
Mrs C. B. Steel, St Andrews, Fife	18, 29b
Mr Stephen Haskell, Greenwich, S.E.10	19a
Mr Mark Palmer, Potters Bar, Herts	19b
Mr G. R. E. Arnot, London, W.11	20a
Mr P. Bradley, Gosforth, Northumberland	20b
Mr J. E. Garfitt, Nailsworth, Glos	21a
Mr Z. I. Buner, London, N.3	21c
Mr L. M. Lipsey, Stroud, Glos	22a
Mr John A. Deft, Cambridge	22b
Mr Lawrence J. Brooks, Braintree, Essex	23a
Mr J. M. Popkin, Headington, Oxford	23b, 23c
Mr Robert T. Barrett, Haverfordwest, Pembs	24a
Miss Julie Brown, Yelverton, S. Devon	24b
Mr Edmund Akenhead, South Newton, Wilts	25a, 57b
Mrs R. J. H. Gillman, Old Burseledon, Hants	26
Mr P. J. Smith, Warrington, Lancs	27a
Mr G. A. Officer, Penkridge, Staffs	27b
Mrs P. D. Bennett, Leamington Spa, Warwicks	28a
Mr E. Corin, Bath, Somerset	28b
Dr David Abbott, Cambridge	29a, 47a, 59b, 78a, 86a, 87a

ACKNOWLEDGEMENTS

Mr D. W. L. Chapman, Harrow, Middx	30
Miss Alison Crawshaw, London, W.2	31a
Mr E. D. Papworth, North Harrow, Middx	31b
Mr Anthony Goode, Exeter, Devon	32a
Miss Amanda Goodman, Hendon, London, N.W.4	32b
Mr Arnold Reuben, Leeds, Yorkshire	33
Mr H. J. Wallis, London, S.E.22	34
The Revd W. M. A. Potts, Newport, I.O.W.	35a
Mr W. G. Williamson, Forest Row, Sussex	35b, 36a
Mr John Higginbotham, Lancing, Sussex	36b
Dr Ronald Pearson, Wirral, Cheshire	37a, 51c
Miss J. M. Richards, Mordiford, Hereford	37b
Miss Vera Burden, Wembley, Middx	38a
Mrs Margaret Barlow, Poole, Dorset	38b
Mr Christopher Perraton, Melksham, Wilts	39a
Mr Alan Bradley, London, W.13	39b
The Revd J. Tolhurst, Croydon, Surrey	40a
Mrs Eleanor M. Sampson, Lingfield, Surrey	40b
Mr M. W. N. Hughes-Hallett, Broadway, Worcs	40c
Mr Gordon H. Leonard, Burnham, Bucks	41a
Mr A. Wiltshire, Leatherhead, Surrey	41b
Mr F. E. Wallwork, Basingstoke, Hants	42a
Mr W. H. F. Butler, Lee-on-the-Solent, Hants	42b
Miss E. M. Wood, Cirencester, Glos	42c, 49a
Longman Group Ltd	43
Mr Jacob C. Thompson, Henley-on-Thames, Berks	44–5
Mrs E. A. Loveridge, Ystradfellte, Glam	46a
Mr Alexander Murray, University of Newcastle upon Tyne	46b, 58
Mr P. R. Dormer, Leeds, Yorks	47b
Mr F. Dellow, Portsmouth, Hants	48a
Mr C. P. Whetton, Swansea, Glam	48b
Miss J. M. E. Payton, London, S.W.13	49b
Professor R. A. Howie, London, W.C.2	50
Dr J. B. P. Williamson, Smethwick Warley, Worcs	51a
Mr C. H. Weeks, Coulsdon, Surrey	51b
Mr C. R. H. Strick, Haywards Heath, Sussex	52a
Miss Dorothy Bisson, London, N.W.7	52b
Miss Dawn MacLeod, Bath, Somerset	53a
Mrs F. Evans, Wimborne, Dorset	54
Brown, Son & Ferguson, Ltd	55a

Mr Raymond Ward, Sheffield, Yorks   55b
Mrs J. L. McCreery, Farnham, Surrey   56a
Mr J. R. Taylor, Newcastle under Lyme, Staffs   56b
Dr Peter H. Mann, Sheffield University   56c
Mr B. A. Woods, Kettering, Northants   57a
Mr D. W. Blandford, Croydon, Surrey   59a
Mr T. E. Annetts, Braintree, Essex   60a
Dr D. J. Pointer, Middlesbrough, Teesside   60b, 64b
Mr V. J. Blackmore, Minehead, Somerset   60c
Mr M. T. McCahill, Leighton Buzzard, Beds   61, 63a
Mr Brian C. Lowe, Reading, Berks   62
Mr Ronald J. Reid, The New University of
    Ulster, Londonderry   63b
Lieut.-Col. A. H. Cox, Cranleigh, Surrey   64a
Mr J. D. Warwick, Chard, Somerset   65
Mr J. Schwiller, Southampton, Hants   66a
Messrs Marcus Sutton & Robert Cade,
    Ashbourne, Derbyshire   66b, 70b
Dr S. J. Branch, Epsom, Surrey   66c–67
Mr Peter Elsdon, Middlesbrough, Teesside   68
Mr J. Derek Bray, Oadby, Leicester   69a, 69c–69d
Rear-Admiral G. I. M. Balfour, Haslemere, Surrey   69b
Mrs W. H. Dyson, Axminster, Devon   70a
Mr Gordon Clarke, Cheadle, Cheshire   71a
Mr D. P. Wood, London, E.C.4   71b
Mr J. R. Lat Corrie, Haslemere, Surrey   72a
Mr Ian D. McAnulla, Ayr, Scotland   72b
Mr Hubert Murray, London, S.E.10   73a, 73b
Professor Michael Gough, University of Toronto   73c
Mr Alfred Austen, New Malden, Surrey   74
Miss Dilys Williams, Newbury, Berks   75a
Mr J. Carter, Bury, Lancs   75b
Mr C. H. Brooks, Headingley, Yorks   76a
Mr Martin S. Wolmark, Bushey Heath, Herts   76b
Mr E. A. C. Chamberlain, Harrow, Middx   76c
Mr B. Willington, Middlesbrough, Teesside   77
Mr A. R. N. Roberts, Tonbridge, Kent   78b
Dr J. P. McLaughlin, Dublin   78c
Mr K. R. E. Smith, Chiselhurst, Kent   78d
Mrs Julian Sandys, London, S.W.7   79a
Mr Stanley J. Oldfield, Twickenham, Middx   79b
Mrs Edith M. Lynch, Potters Bar, Herts   79c

ACKNOWLEDGEMENTS

Mr Stanley H. Hodgson, Bridport, Dorset	80a
Mr C. K. Elliott, Ilkley, Yorks	80b
Miss Janet Seamons, London, S.E.6	81
Mrs Peter Moore, Hadley Wood, Herts	82a
Mrs Dorothy Diamond, London, W.3	82b
Mrs R. Scott, Stockport, Cheshire	83a
Mr John Field, Cookham, Berkshire	83b
W. & M. Kneale, *The Development of Logic*, Oxford, The Clarendon Press (1962)	84
The Monotype Corporation and Mr Arthur Phillips	85
Mr G. L. Lilly, Crosby, Isle of Man	86b
Professor Luciano Bologna, Torino, Italy	87a
Mr Robert L. Bayne-Powell, Borough Green, Kent	87b
Dr A. Hayward, Glasgow	88
Mr E. J. Bowen, Oxford	89
Miss Phyllis Jones, Buckfastleigh, Devon	90
Mrs B. E. Ratzer, Chaldon, Surrey	91a
Sir Ralph Windham, Ongar, Essex	91b

Acids, amino

For the ten essential amino acids (arginine and histidine only required by infants) :

These **t**en **v**aluable **a**mino-acids **h**ave **l**ong **p**reserved **l**ife **i**n **m**an.

(threonine, tryptophan, valine, arginine, histidine, lysine, phenylalanine, leucine, isoleucine, methionine)

Acids, di-carboxylic

For the first seven members cf the series :

Only **m**en **s**eek **g**irls **as p**iquant **s**pouses.

(oxalic, malonic, succinic, glutaric, adipic, pimelic, suberic)

Alternative

(for the first six only) :

Omsgap

(oxalic, malonic, succinic, glutaric, adipic, pimelic)

Algebra

For the order of operations in complex algebraic or numerical expression:

Bless **m**y **d**ear **A**unt **S**ally!

(brackets, multiply, divide, add, subtract)

Arteries in frog

For the arteries in a frog, in the order in which they branch off the main aorta:

Little **m**en **i**n **s**hort **b**lack **m**ackintoshes.

(lingual, mandibular, innominate, subclavian, brachial, musculocutaneous)

Atom, model of

For the order in which shells are filled in the
quantum mechanical model of the atom:

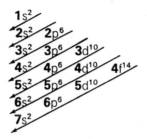

(i.e. the order follows that of the arrows downwards
from the top:

$1s^2$ $2s^2$ $2p^6$ $3s^2$ $3p^6$ $4s^2$ $3d^{10}$ $4p^6$ $5s^2$
$4d^{10}$ $5p^6$ $6s^2$ $4f^{14}$ $5d^{10}$ $6p^6$ $7s^2$)

Battles, dates of

For those in the War of the Spanish Succession,
use 'the Duke of Marlborough's telephone number':

BROM 4689

(**B**lenheim 170**4**, **R**amillies 170**6**, **O**udenarde 170**8**,
Malplaquet 170**9**)

For an assorted trio:

Think of

13B, 14A, 15F

as in a triangle, which gives 'Bannockburn 1314',
'Agincourt 1415', 'Flodden 1513'.

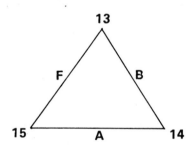

Bile

For the properties of bile:

Bile from the liver emulsifies greases
Tinges the urine and colours the faeces
Aids peristalsis, prevents putrefaction
If you remember all this you'll give satisfaction.

Blood

For the functions of the blood:

Old **C**harlie **F**oster **h**ates **w**omen **h**aving **d**ull **c**lothes.

(oxygen (transport), carbon dioxide (transport), food, heat, waste, hormones, disease, clotting)

Bones

For the bones of the upper limb:

Some **c**riminals **h**ave **u**nderestimated **R**oyal **C**anadian **M**ounted **P**olice.

(scapula, clavicle, humerus, ulna, radius, carpals, metacarpals, phalanges)

For the bones of the lower limb:

Help **f**or **p**olice **t**o **f**ind **t**he **m**issing **p**risoner.

(hip, femur, patella, tibia, fibula, tarsals, metatarsals, phalanges)

For the vertebral bones of the spinal column:

Clever **D**ick **l**ooks **s**illy **c**lot.

(cervical, dorsal, lumbar, sacrum, coccyx)

Caesar, battles won by

For his victories in the struggle with Pompey's faction (49–45 B.C.):

Is perpetual zeal the means?

(Ilerda, Pharsalus, Zela, Thapsus, Munda)

Camels

For distinguishing two species:

A camel I am it's plain to see
But am I a Bactrian or Dromedary?
Lay down the ⋒ and then the ⌂
And which I am is plain as can be.

ABCDEFGHIJKLMNOPQRSTUVWXYZ

Carbohydrates, monosaccharides

For the eight D-aldohexoses (a series of sugars containing six carbon atoms) :

All **a**ltruists **g**ladly **m**ake **g**um **i**n **g**allon **t**anks.

(Allose, altrose, glucose, mannose, gulose, idose, galactose, talose)

Cataloguing

For one order (not that of the 1967 Library Association code) in which to list illustration details in the collation catalogue entry for a book:

Flirting **i**ll-**p**leases **p**arents **p**ursuing **m**atrimonial **p**lans **f**or **t**heir **d**aughters.

(frontispiece, illustrations, plates, photographs, portraits, maps, plans, facsimiles, tables, diagrams)

ABCDEFGHIJKLMNOPQRSTUVWXYZ

Cedars

For distinguishing the three common British
species of cedar:

Atlas cedar has generally **a**scending branches;
Lebanon has generally **l**evel branches;
Deodar has generally **d**rooping branches.

Cell division

For the stages in mitosis and meiosis, the types of
cell division:

Mitosis **P**eas **m**ake **a**wful **t**arts.
(prophase, metaphase, anaphase, telophase)

Meiosis **L**azy **Z**ulus **p**ursue **d**ark **d**amsels.
(leptotene, zygotene, pachytene, diplotene,
diakinesis)

Alternative

for mitosis:

In **P**ersia **m**en **a**re **t**all.

(interphase, prophase, metaphase, anaphase,
telophase)

21

Children

For checking items in making them presentable:

Hideous **f**ools and **m**orons, **k**eep **s**ilent!

(H = hair brushed?
 f = face washed?
 m = middle (i.e. shirt tucked in, or belt on)?
 k = knees clean?
 s = shoes tied (brushed)?)

Circle

For circumference and area:

Fiddlededum, fiddlededee,
A ring round the moon is π times d,
If a hole in your sock you want repaired,
You use the formula πr squared.

Circuit

For the order of items in an A.C. circuit:

The **voltage** (V) across a **capacitor** (C) lags the **current** (I) by 90 degrees. The voltage across the **inductor** (L) leads the current by 90 degrees. This is given by the word CIVIL, when split into CIV and VIL.

Classification

For the order of taxonomic classification:

Krakatoa **p**ositively **c**asts **o**ff **f**umes **g**enerating **s**ulphurous **v**apours.

(Kingdom, phylum, class, order, family, genus, species, variety)

Alternative

Kindly **p**lace **c**over **o**n **f**resh **g**reen **s**pring **v**egetables.

Classification

For the geological periods in descending order of age:

Camels **o**ften **s**it **d**own **c**arefully. **P**erhaps
their **j**oints **c**reak? **E**arly **o**iling **m**ight
prevent **p**ermanent **r**heumatism.

(Cambrian, Ordovician, Silurian, Devonian,
Carboniferous, Permian, Triassic, Jurassic,
Cretaceous, Eocene, Oligocene, Miocene,
Pliocene, Pleistocene, Recent)

Alternative

China **o**wls **s**eldom **d**eceive **c**lay **p**igeons. **T**hey
just **c**hase **e**ach **o**ther **m**aking **p**reposterous **p**uns.

Days in month

For the number in each of the twelve months:

Hold one clenched hand before you, knuckles up.
With the finger of the other hand tap the
knuckle of the first finger and say 'January' –
tap the valley between that and the next
knuckle and say 'February'. Continue to July
which will be the last knuckle and then go
back to the first knuckle for August,
continuing to December.

All the 'knuckle' months have 31 days.

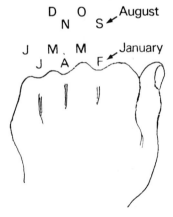

Alternative

Thirty days hath September
April, June, and November.
All the rest have thirty-one
Excepting February alone
Which has twenty-eight days clear
And twenty-nine in each leap year.

ABC**D**EFGHIJKLMNOPQRSTUVWXYZ

Drink

For avoiding hangover:

Beer on whisky very risky.
Whisky on beer never fear.

Electrochemical series

[*Electromotive series*]

For the elements in their correct order:

Poorly **c**anned **s**ausages **m**ake **a Z**ulu **i**ll, **t**herefore
let **h**ighly **c**lever **m**en **s**lay **g**ood **p**igs.

(Potassium, calcium, sodium, magnesium,
aluminium, zinc, iron, tin, lead, hydrogen,
copper, mercury, silver, gold, platinum.
[K,Ca,Na,Mg,Al,Zn,Fe,Sn,Pd,H,Cu,Hg,Ag,Au,Pt])

Alternative

This gives the order referred to electrode
potential, which gives a slightly different
arrangement than for reactivity as regards
sodium and silver; lithium is placed before
potassium and gold is at the end:

Little **K**atie **c**an **n**ever **m**ake **a z**ip **f**it **s**kirts
properly, **h**er **c**lothes **a**lways **h**ang **a**wkwardly.

(Li,K,Ca,Na,Mg,Al,Zn,Fe,Sn,Pb,H,Cu,Ag,Hg,Au)

Emperors, Roman

For some of them, in order:

> **A**t **t**he **C**anine **C**lub **n**ever **g**ive **o**ut **v**iscous
> **v**egetables **t**o **d**almatians.

(Augustus, Tiberius, Caligula, Claudius, Nero,
Galba, Otho, Vitellius, Vespasian, Titus, Domitian)

Alternative

> **A** **t**rue **C**onservative **c**an **n**ot **gov**ern **v**irtuously:
> **t**hey **d**o **n**ot **t**hemselves **h**ate **a**varice **a**ltogether.

(Augustus; Tiberius; Caligula; Claudius;
Nero; Galba, Otho, Vitellius (same year);
Vespasian; Titus; Domitian; Nerva; Trajan;
Hadrian; Antoninus Pius; Aurelius (Marcus))

Enzymes

For the classification of enzymes according to their type of action in biochemistry:

Hot in Africa

(hydrolases, oxidoreductases, transferases, isomerases, additives)

Excretion

For the excretory organs of the body:

Skill

(skin, kidneys, intestines, liver, lungs)

Filters, colour

For the colour filter to use on a camera:

There are three primary colours, yellow, red,
and blue,
Any one of which 'holds back' the other two.

(So a yellow filter suppresses both red and blue
light etc.)

Fleming's rule

For identifying direction of magnetic field, electrical current, and motion:

Hold left hand with thumb, first and second fingers mutually at right angles. Then the mnemonic:

Centre, current
First for field
Then the thu**m**b will motion yield.

gives direction.

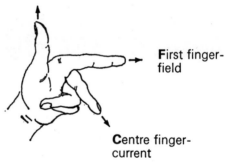

Use the right hand for dynamos.

Reminder (for hand)

D is for **D**ad and for **D**ynamos; **M** is for **M**um and for **M**otors. **D**ad is always right.

Fossils, zonal index

For the names of the zonal index fossils of
part of the lower Carboniferous System of
Great Britain:

   King **Z**og **c**aught **s**yphilis and **d**ied.

This refers to the k, z, c, s and d zones which
acquire their initials from the fossil names
Cleistopora, Zaphrentis, Caninia, Seminula and
Dibunophylum. As two of these have the initial c,
geologists decided to call the lowest zone k.

Fractions

For the rule of division of fractions:

   The number you are dividing by
   Turn upside down and multiply.

French grammar

For the adjectives which precede their nouns:

Bon, mauvais, méchant, sot,
Grand, petit, vaste, haut,
Vilain, jeune, vieux, beau,
Ancien, long, joli, gros,
Digne, cher, saint, nouveau

For verbs which are compounded with *être*
in the perfect tense:

Aller, arriver, monter, venir,
Entrer, rester, demeurer, partir,
Descendre, tomber, retourner, sortir,
Naître, décéder, devenir, mourir.

For those nouns ending in -ou which take the
plural ending -x:

Mes choux, mes bijoux,
Laissez vos joujoux,
Venez sur mes genoux!
Regardez ces mauvais petits garçons
Qui jettent des cailloux à ces pauvres hiboux!

Glass, fracturing of

For identifying the cause of a breakage:

Rrr

When glass is broken by a blow, the broken edges show curved stress marks. On broken edges radiating from the point of impact (radial cracks), these marks are invariably asympototic to the surface of the glass on which the blow was delivered, and approximately perpendicular to the other surface. This fact is important to the forensic scientist who has to determine whether the window was broken from the outside or the inside. Hence:

Radial **r**ight-angles **r**everse.

Greek

For the construction of vowels in endings of
Present stem forms of classical Greek -ω
verbs whose stems end in α and ο:

Little α wins the day
Except when ο gets in the way
(for -αω verbs);
Short vowel ου, long vowel ω
Anything with ι into οι will go
(for -οω verbs).

Alternative

A with any kind of O
into Omega will go:
with any vowel else will stay
simply as a lengthened A.
Iota you must always show
subscript written down below.
E before anything lengthy will fly;
with O becomes OU and with E becomes EI.
Please remember this, my boy,
that O with any I makes OI.
For O with any vowel long
Omega will not be wrong.
All the rest is easy now,
for O with anything else makes OU.

Greek prepositions

For cases governed by these:

ἀντί, ἀπό, ἐκ and πρό
with the GENITIVE do go.
ἐν and σύν must have the DATIVE
εἰς, ὡς, ἀνά – ACCUSATIVE.
διά, κατά, ὑπέρ, μετά
have two cases, don't forget!
ἐπί, παρά, and περί (round)
ὑπό and πρός with three are found.

Greek verbs

For the important distinction between φαίνομαι
and infinitive (I appear to be – but in reality I am
not) and φαίνομαι and participle (I clearly am):

φαίνομαι ὤν – quod sum,
quod non sum – φαίνομαι εἶναι.

Harmonics, simple

For the periodic time of a simple pendulum:

> The wonders of Nature, quoth he,
> Are always a marvel to me:
> That each tick and a tock
> of a grandfather clock
> is $2\pi\sqrt{\dfrac{l}{g}}$ (two pi root **l** over **g**).

Henry VIII

For the successive fates of his wives
(Catherine of Aragon, Anne Boleyn, Jane Seymour,
Anne of Cleves, Catherine Howard, Catherine Parr):

> Divorced, beheaded, died;
> divorced, beheaded, survived.

Houses, Royal

For the order of English and British ruling houses:

No **p**lan **l**ike **y**ours **t**o **s**tudy **h**istory **w**isely.

(Norman, Plantaganet, Lancaster, York, Tudor, Stuart, Hanover, Windsor)

Inertia matrix

For the order of items in the matrix:

A	H	G
H	B	F
G	F	C

A **h**airy **g**orilla **h**as **b**ig **f**eet, **g**ood **f**or climbing.

where A, B, C are the moments and H, F, G are the products of inertia.

Insects

For the parts of an insect's leg:

Cockroaches **t**ravel **f**ast **t**owards **t**heir **c**hildren.

(Coxa, trochanter, femur, tibia, tarsus, claw)

Integration

Hardy's formula for approximate integration:

To remember a number is to be a strong or hardy person. I always do.

This is much used by actuaries, and relates to the numerical coefficients in the formula

$$\int_0^\infty U t\, dt = (\cdot 28U_0 + 1\cdot 62U_n + 2\cdot 2U_{3n} + 1\cdot 62U_{5n} + \cdot 56U_{6n} + 1\cdot 62U_{7n})_n$$

Kings and Queens

For their order, from William the Conqueror:

Willie, Willie, Harry, Stee,
Harry, Dick, John, Harry Three,
One, Two, Three Neds, Richard Two,
Harry Four, Five, Six. Then who?
Edward Four, Five, Dick the Bad,
Harrys twain and Ned the Lad,
Mary, Bessie, James the Vain,
Charlie, Charlie, James again,
William and Mary, Anna Gloria,
Four Georges, William, and Victoria.

Alternative:

When will his stupid head remember
Just how easy each endeavour
Remains, having had help;
Eclipsing every reasoning, harassing, hazy,
    egotist's method,
Elaborately jumbling clear concise junctures
With a great grand gravity giving wit vexation.

Another updated alternative to the first one continues:

Edward Seventh next, and then
George the Fifth in 1910.
Edward the Eighth soon abdicated
And so a George was reinstated.

Kirchhoff's laws

For solving complex electrical circuits:

A student under a stigma
Once chanced to remember that sigma
CR's = E's and nought equals C's,
Thus solving his little enigma.

Lakes, the Great

For their west-to-east order:

Sergeant-**M**ajor **h**ates **e**ating **o**nions.

(Superior, Michigan, Huron, Erie, Ontario)

ABCDEFGHIJ**KL**MNOPQRSTUVWXYZ

Latin

For the meanings of the stem 'mal-':

Malo – I would rather be
Malo – in an apple tree
Malo – than a wicked man
Malo – in adversity.

For the (irregular) active imperative singular of the
verbs dicere, ducere, ferre, facere:

Dic(k) had a **duc**(k) with fur (**fer**) on its back,
and that's a **fac**(t).

For the declension of 'domus', which has mixed
2nd and 4th declension endings:

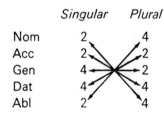

(note that the numbers 'match' with arrowed straight
lines)

Latin gender rhymes

For general guidance:

A Man, a name of People and a Wind,
River and Mountain, masculine we find:
Romulus, Hispani, Zephyrus, Cocytus, Olympus.

A Woman, Island, Country, Tree,
and City, feminine we see:
Penelope, Cyprus, Germania, laurus, Athenae.

To nouns that cannot be declined
the neuter gender is assigned:
Examples *fas* and *nefas* give
And the verb-noun infinitive:
Est summum nefas fallere:
Deceit is gross impiety.

(There are plenty more special declension-rules in
Kennedy's *Shorter Latin Primer,* source of the above,
but exceptions to them are many and can invalidate
learning the mnemonic.)

Latin jingles

For declension of nouns:

As MAN to BOY I'd like to mention
VIR and PUER are SECOND Declension.

No wonder that his eyeballs blaze
at FLUMINEM or FLUMINES!
(-MEN, -MINIS NEUTER)

The GENDER of FLOWER and of TREE
in French and Latin disagree.
(FLEUR, fem. ARBRE, masc.
FLOS, masc. ARBOR, fem.)

For the formation of verbs:

He throws a fit
of righteous wrath,
at -BO, -BIS, -BIT
in 3rd or 4th.

PRESENT SUBJUNCTIVES,
I can't forget them.
They're all -AM, except AMO
and AMO's AMEM.

Caesar was right, though rather cheeky,
in saying, 'VENI. VIDI. VICI.'
Any boy is wrong who thinks he
said, 'VENIVI. VISI. VINXI.'

For various syntax-points:

I've probably put my great flat foot in it,
if I've written a sentence with 'DICO UT' in it.

An INDIRECT STATEMENT we have to append
to 'HOPE', 'PROMISE', 'THREATEN', 'SWEAR',
   and 'PRETEND'.
'I'm afraid of the sea;' is 'Timeo MARE.'
'I'm afraid to give that' is 'Id timeo DARE.'
'Timeo NE SIT calidum' . . . 'I fear that
   it's hot.'
The same with NE NON is 'I fear that it's not.'

INDICATIVE must go,
with 'QUAMQUAM' . . . 'ALTHOUGH'.
The moral of this
is 'Beware of QUAMVIS'.

You may employ SUPINE in -UM
for PURPOSE after 'SEND' or 'COME'.
'Matrem VISUM exierunt.'
'They've gone out to see their parent.'

SUPINE in -U
'Easy to do.'
'Facile FACTU.'

ABCDEFGHIJKLMNOPQRSTUVWXYZ

Latin verbs

For common verbs which govern the dative case:

A Dative put, remember, pray,
After envy, spare, obey
Persuade, believe, command – to these
Add pardon, succour and displease.
With vacare, to have leisure
Add placere, to give pleasure,
With nubere, of the female said:
The English of it is 'to wed'.
Servire add and add studere
Favour, resist and indulgere.

Liberal arts, the seven

For the three 'verbal' arts studied in the *trivium* and
the four 'real' arts of the *quadrivium*:

These appear in lines one and two respectively of
the medieval mnemonic:

Gram loquitur, **Dia** vera docet, **Rhe** verba colorat,
Mus canit, **Ar** numerat, **Geo** ponderat, **As** colit
astra.

(Gram(-mar) speaks, Dia(-lectic) teaches truths,
        Rhe(-toric) gives colour to words,
Mus(-ic) sings, Ar(-ithmetic) counts, Geo(-metry)
    takes measure, As(-tronomy) studies the stars.)

Living things

For the major characteristics of living organisms:

Newmarket **r**uns **e**very **g**reat **r**ace **i**n **M**ay.

[nutrition, respiration, excretion, growth, reproduction, irritability (response to conditions), movement]

Logarithms, Naperian

For the base of Naperian (or Natural) logarithms:

To express '**e**', remember to memorise a sentence to simplify this.

(2.7182818284)

Machines

For the definition of mechanical advantage $= \dfrac{\text{load}}{\text{effort}}$:

Men **a**lways **l**ike **e**ating.

Maxwell equations

For the thermodynamic relationships, using the Standard abbreviations t = absolute temperature, P = absolute pressure, v = specific volume, s = specific entropy (and with the word 'may' standing for a minus sign):

Two vergers singing may Please some vicars

$$\left(\frac{\partial t}{\partial v}\right)_s = -\left(\frac{\partial P}{\partial s}\right)_v$$

Ten People sang very soft Psalms

$$\left(\frac{\partial t}{\partial P}\right)_s = \left(\frac{\partial v}{\partial s}\right)_P$$

Peter's tiny vole sings very tenderly

$$\left(\frac{\partial P}{\partial t}\right)_v = \left(\frac{\partial s}{\partial v}\right)_t$$

Voles talking Persian may sound Pretty terrible

$$\left(\frac{\partial v}{\partial t}\right)_P = -\left(\frac{\partial s}{\partial P}\right)_t$$

Metre, classical

For examples of one each of hexameter, pentameter, and hendecasyllabic verse metres:

Dówn in a | déep dárk | déll sat an |
old cow | múnching a | béanstalk.

While in the | múd néar | by ||
wállowed a | lítter of | pígs.

Só fán | -tástical | ís the | dáinty | métre.

Metric weights and measures

For the descending order of scale:

Kippers **h**ardly **d**are **m**ove **d**uring **c**old **m**onths.

(Kilometre, Hectometre, Dekametre, Metre, decimetre, centimetre, millimetre)

Alternative

King **H**enry **d**ied – **m**other/**g**ranny **d**idn't **c**are **m**uch.

(in which 'm/g' may stand for either metres or grams, throughout)

Minerals

For the order of formation of calc-silicate minerals on the contact metamorphism of a siliceous dolomite :

Tall **t**rees **d**on't **f**all **w**hen **P**luto **m**akes a**tt**empts **t**o **s**hake **r**ock **m**asses **l**oose.

(Talc, tremolite, dolomite, forsterite, wollastonite, periclase, monticellite, akernite, tilleyite, spurrite, rankinite, merwinite, larnite)

MOH, scale of

For the order of hardness:

Tall **g**yroscopes **c**an **fl**y **a**part, **or**bitting **qu**ickly
to complete **di**sintegration.

(talc, gypsum or rock salt, calcite, fluorite, apatite,
orthaclase, quartz, topaz, corondum, diamond)

Alternative

Those **g**irls **c**an **fl**irt **an**d **o**ther **qu**eer **th**ings
can **d**o.

Momentum

Momentum and impulse *pt*
Are vectors which oft troubled me.
But momentum I state,
In seconds/pounds weight,
is $\dfrac{wv}{g}$.

Month, first days of

For the day of the week on which the 1st of each
month falls:

> **A**t **D**over **d**welt **G**eorge **B**rown, **E**squire,
> **G**ood **C**hristopher **F**inch, **a**nd **D**avid **F**ryer.

Thus, in 1971 the first of January fell on a Friday
(represented by 'At' in the mnemonic). The first day
of July will be represented by the seventh word,
'Good'. G is six letters after A in the alphabet, six
days after Friday would be Thursday, therefore the
1st of July was a Thursday.

In leap years, one extra day has to be added to the
calculation for all months after February.

Medieval alternatives (for the 'ferial' days of the
church calendar):

> **A**ltitonans **d**ominus **d**ivina **g**erens **b**onus **e**xtat:
> **G**ratuito **c**eli **f**ert **a**urea **d**ona **f**ideli.

> **A**lta **d**omat **d**ominus; **g**ratis **b**eat **e**qua **g**erentes,
> **C**ontemnit **f**ictos, **a**ugebit **d**ona **f**ideli.

Moon

For distinguishing waning from waxing:

If its crescent fits the natural curve of the right hand (**ɔ**) then it is *Increasing* (the 'right' has an 'i'). The curve of the *left* hand (**C**) fits a *dEcreasing* moon ('left' has an 'e').

A 'negative alternative'

When it is Coming (**ɑ**) it is really Departing.
When it is Departing (**D**) it is really Coming.

Morse code

For learning the allocation of Morse dots and dashes to letters of the alphabet:

A
.—
Alone

B
—...
beautifully

C
—.—.
come a cropper

D
—..
daintily

E
.
egg

F
..—.
for a fortnight

G
——.
good gracious

H
....
ha ha ha ha

I
..
is it?

J
.———
Japan's jam jars

K
—.—
Kiss me Kate

L
.—..
linoleum

M
——
my mate

N
—.
naughty

O
———
our old oak

P
.——.
polite person

Q
——.—
quite queer & quaint

R
.—.
rewarding

S
...
sh sh sh

T
—
tea

U
..—
underneath

V
...—
very verbose

W
.——
without waste

X
—..—
extra expense

Y
—.——
yellow yacht's yarn

Z
——..
zeb-zeb-ra-ra

Alternative

A   **B**   **C**   **D**
.—   —...   —.—.   —..
Ahoy   bountifully   correspondent   doubtfully

E   **F**   **G**   **H**
.   ..—.   ——.   ....
ek   for as much as   good graces   he he he he

I   **J**   **K**
..   .———   —.—
Impi   Japan black juice   kingdom come

L   **M**   **N**   **O**
.—..   ——   —.   ———
litigious   moonshine   needy   onoto

P   **Q**   **R**
.——.   ——.—   .—.
prepare paper   queen's quietude   regardless

S   **T**   **U**   **V**
...   —   ..—   ...—
sisterly   tow   uninformed   vivificate

W   **X**   **Y**
.——   —..—   —.——
without work   extra extent   yearly yulelog

Z
——..
zoological

Footnote on '**SOS**':

The international distress signal 'SOS' is a form of mnemonic in that it was chosen because in Morse code it is simply dot dot dot, dash dash dash, dot dot dot — easy to remember, transmit, receive and recognise. It does not stand for 'Save our souls' or anything else.

Navigation

For night steering:

If to your starboard Red appear
It is your duty to keep clear.
Green to Green or Red to Red
In perfect safety go ahead.

Alternative

When both lights you see ahead
Starboard your wheel (Or 'Port your helm')
And show your red.

Navigation lights, colour

For placing these correctly:

Port wine should be **left** alone when it is **red**.

Nerves

For the order of nerves that pass through the superior orbital tissue in the skull:

Lazy **F**rench **t**arts **l**ie **n**aked **i**n **a**nticipation.

(lacrinal, frontal, trochlear, lateral, nasociliary, internal, abduceir)

Nones, Ides

For dating these in the Roman calendar:

March, July, October, May
Have Nones the 7th, Ides the 15th, day.

(Those of other months come two days earlier, 5th and 13th.)

Notes, musical

For the names of the scale:

A medieval mnemonic for the names of notes rising
upwards in the diatonic scale was taught by
Guido of Arezzo (d. 1050). He named each note
after a syllable of a familiar hymn (to Saint John
Baptist), each such syllable opening a line:

(So that your servants may, with bursting lungs,
resound the wonders of your deeds, cleanse the
sin of unclean lips, O Saint John.)

Ti and *do* were later additions.

Numerals, Roman

For their values:

X shall stand for playmates Ten,
V for Five stout stalwart men,
I for One, as I'm alive,
C for Hundred and **D** for Five,
M for a Thousand soldiers true,
and **L** for Fifty, I'll tell you.

Nutrition

For the classification of feeding methods:

All **c**ounty **p**layers **h**ave **h**undreds of **s**hots **p**erfected

(autotrophic [i chemosynthetic ii photosynthetic], heterotrophic [i holozoic ii saprophytic iii parasitic])

ABCDEFGHIJKLMN**O**PQRSTUVWXYZ

Ohm

For the order of ohmic values in resistors:

Billy **B**rown **r**elies **o**n **y**our **g**in **b**ut **p**refers **g**ood **w**hisky.

(black, brown, red, orange, yellow, green, blue, purple, grey, white)

Alternative

Where the purple coding is seen as violet:

Bye **b**ye **R**osie, **o**ff **y**ou **g**o: **B**irmingham **v**ia **G**reat **W**estern.

Another alternative

Better **b**e **r**ight **o**r **y**our **g**reat **b**ig **v**enture **g**oes **w**est.

Ohm's law

For one expression of this:

Virgins **a**re **r**are.

(Volts = amps × resistance)

Old Testament

For the order of its books:

The great Jehovah speaks to us
In Genesis and Exodus;
Leviticus and Numbers see,
Followed by Deuteronomy.
Joshua and Judges sway the land
Ruth gleans a sheaf with trembling hand:
Samuel and numerous Kings appear,
Whose Chronicles we wondering hear.
Ezra and Nehemiah now,
Esther, the beauteous mourner show,
Job speak in sighs, David in Psalms,
The Proverbs teach to scatter alms.
Ecclesiastes then comes on,
And the sweet Song of Solomon.
Isaiah, Jeremiah then,
With Lamentations takes his pen,
Ezekiel, Daniel, Hosea's lyres,
Swell Joel, Amos, Obadiah's.
Next Jonah, Micah, Nahum come,
And lofty Habakkuk finds room.
While Zephaniah, Haggai calls,
Rapt Zechariah builds his walls,
And Malachi, with garments rent,
CONCLUDES THE ANCIENT TESTAMENT....

Optics

For the additive and subtractive mixtures of colours:

Better **g**et **r**eady **w**hile
Your **m**istress **c**omes **b**ack.

[Blue + green + red = white (additive)
yellow + magenta + cyan = black (subtractive)]

Orbitals

For their order:

Spin **p**airs **d**on't **f**orm – **g**o **h**igher.

The Pauli selection rule states that two electrons of
like spin may not be present in any orbital if they
have the same set of quantum numbers.   Since the
electronic orbitals in atoms are listed by the letters
s, p, d, f, g, h, in order of ascending energy, the
mnemonic reminds.

Orders, military

For the sequence of items in giving orders:

11 MAI

(information, intention, method, administration, intercommunication)

Organic chemistry

[*Sandmeyer's reaction*]

For the transformation of a primary aromatic amine into the corresponding halogen (usually bromine) compound using copper (I) bromide as a catalyst:

Traugot Sandmeyer
Made his reputation stand fire
Using Cu_2Br_2
For getting Br out of NH_2

Pascal's triangle

For the coefficients in expansions:

In mathematics we often need to expand a
function such as $(1 + x)^6$. We know that the
answer will contain a certain number of x^6, x^5, x^4,
x^3 etc but if we cannot remember the coefficients
it means multiplying the bracket out six times.
Pascal's triangle is of the form

$$
\begin{array}{ccccccc}
 & & & 1 & & 1 & \\
 & & 1 & & 2 & & 1 \\
 & 1 & & 3 & & 3 & & 1 \\
1 & & 4 & & 6 & & 4 & & 1 \\
1 & 5 & & 10 & & 10 & & 5 & & 1
\end{array}
$$
etc.

The next line is produced by adding two
consecutive numbers together and putting
the answer on the next line.

Hence to find the terms of $(1 + x)^6$ we require
the sixth line of Pascal's triangle which is
1, 6, 15, 20, 15, 6, 1. Hence $(1 + x)^6 =$
$1 + 6x + 15x^2 + 20x^3 + 15x^4 + 6x^5 + x^6$.

Periodic table

For the elements in their correct order in the first three periods of the table (hydrogen being omitted and potassium included) :

Here **li**es **Be**njamin **B**old **c**ry **n**ot **o**ld **f**riend **ne**edlessly **Na**ture **m**agnifies **al**l **si**mple **p**eople **s**ometimes, **cl**ots and **k**ings.

(hydrogen, helium, lithium, beryllium, boron, carbon, nitrogen, oxygen, fluorine, neon, sodium, magnesium, aluminium, silicon, phosphorus, sulphur, chlorine, argon, potassium. [H, He, Li, Be, B, C, N, O, F, Ne, Na, Mg, Al, Si, P, S, Cl, A, K]).

For the rare earth elements in the chemical periodic table :

Last **ce**ntury **pr**oduced **n**ew **pr**omises **s**anctimoniously. **Eu**rope **g**rows **t**urbulent. **Dy**namic **ho**lidays **er**adicate **t**horoughly **y**our **lu**mbago.

(Lanthanum, Cerium, Praeseodymium, Neodymium, Promethium, Samarium, Europium, Gadolinium, Terbium, Dysprosium, Holmium, Erbium, Thulium, Ytterbium, Lutecium/Lutetium)

For the rare gases : (Group O) :

Heaven **ne**ver **a**sked **Kr**iegspiel's **e**x**t**ra **r**ent.

(Helium, Neon, Argon, Krypton, Xenon, Radon)

Alternative

He neared **a kr**yptic **z**enana **r**uin.

For elements 1–10:

Hell, **h**ere **li**ttle **b**eatniks **b**randish **c**ountless **n**umbers **o**f **f**lick-knive**s**.

For elements Na–A:

Nagging **Ma**ggie **al**ways **s**ips **cl**aret.

For elements Cs–Re:

Cow**s** **b**ear **lar**ger **h**eifers **t**han **w**e **re**alise.

For elements Au–Po:

Audacious **h**ags **s**tealing **p**lead **b**itter **po**verty.

For elements Th–Md:

Though **p**arsons **u**se **na**pkins **pu**ny **Am**ericans **c**onsume **b**lac**k** **c**offees **f**rom maids.

For elements 86 onwards:

Renounce, **fr**ustrated **Al**chemist, **th**is **p**atently **unp**opular **a**tomic **c**onundrum! **Bl**ockheads **c**an't **f**ind **el**ement **f**orms **m**nemonically vali**d**.

The most sustained mnemonic for the elements from Pd onwards is:

Pedestrians, **ag**ilely **c**udgelled **in**sensate **s**ink **su**bmissively, **te**rribly **i**njured. **Xe**nophobic **c**osh-boys **ba**refacedly **l**and **h**efty **t**akings **w**hile **re**sidents, **o**stentatiously **i**rate, **p**etition **a**uthority. **H**igh-level **t**alks **p**ublicly **b**illed. **P**olice **a**ttack. **R**ing-leader, **fr**antic, **ac**ts **th**oughtlessly. **P**atrols **u**nconquerable!

Phenols

For the common names of the dihydric phenols:

Ortho = Cathechol   Organic Chemistry
Meta = Resorcinol   Mister (MR)
Para = Hydroquinone pH (well known in
                              chemistry as potential
                              of hydrogen ion)

Pi [π]

For its numbers (to 30 places) :

Que j'aime à faire apprendre ce nombre utile
aux sages. Immortel Archimède antique, ingénieur.
Qui de ton jugement peut sonder la valeur ? Pour
moi ton problème eut de pareils avantages.
(3·141592653589793238462643383279)

(to 20 places) :

Sir, I send a rhyme excelling
In sacred truth and rigid spelling ;
Numerical sprites elucidate
For me the lexicons dull weight.
(3·14159265358979323846)

(to 14 places) :

How I want a drink, alcoholic of course, after
the heavy chapters involving quantum mechanics.
(3·14159265358979)

For the reciprocal of pi :

Can I remember the reciprocal ?
(0 · 3 1   8   3   10)

ABCDEFGHIJKLMNO**P**QRSTUVWXYZ

Plagues, of Egypt

For their order:

Retaliating **f**or **l**ong **f**rustration **M**oses
badgered **h**ostile **l**eader **d**emanding **f**reedom.

(River to blood, frogs, lice, flies, murrain, boils, hail,
locusts, darkness, first-born)

Planets

For their order, outwards from the Sun:

Men **v**ery **e**asily **m**ake **j**ugs **s**erve **u**seful
nocturnal **p**urposes.

(Mercury, Venus, Earth, Mars, Jupiter, Saturn,
Uranus, Neptune, Pluto)

Poisson formula

For the formula of the Poisson distribution in statistics, the word 'mnemonic' itself. Thus:

$$\frac{m^n e^{-n}}{n!}$$

Or, **m** to the **n**, **e** to the **m**inus n, **o**ver **n** factorial. The 'i' in mnemonic serves as an inverted factorial sign.

Quarter days

For the four days in the four months concerned:

March   — 25th (five letters in 'March')
June   — 24th (four letters in 'June')
September — 29th (nine letters in 'September')

— and if you can't remember Christmas, then you probably shouldn't be in business.

ABCDEFGHIJKLMNOPQ**R**STUVWXYZ

Rahukalam

For the starting-time of the Indian ninety-minute 'auspicious period for new undertakings' (such as setting out on a journey, signing contracts, meeting new people), which repeats on a seven-day cycle:

English **b**oys **h**ave **a** **g**ood **f**ootball **c**lub.

(E = 5th letter. Take half its value and add to full value = 7½. Therefore, on Mondays *rahukalam* runs from 7.30 to 9.00 a.m. Repeat process for remaining days.)

Redox

For the way in which electrons are exchanged in oxidation and reduction:

LEO
(Lose Electrons Oxidation)

GER
(Gain Electrons Reduction)

RAO
(Reducing Agents Oxidised)

OAR
(Oxidising Agents Reduced)

Roads, British

For the first six trunk roads, outwards from London:

Every **d**ay **p**lease **o**bey the **H**ighway **C**ode.

(Al – Edinburgh, A2 – Dover, A3 – Portsmouth,
A4 – Bristol, A5 – Holyhead, A6 – Carlisle)

For the first six motorways (England & Wales):

You'd **m**uch **b**etter **n**ot **b**y **c**ar.

(M1 – Yorkshire, M2 – Medway Towns,
M3 – Basingstoke, M4 – Newport,
M5 – Birmingham–Bristol,
M6 – Birmingham–Carlisle)

Rome, Seven Hills of

For their names:

Can **Q**ueen **V**ictoria **e**at **c**old **a**pple **p**ie?

(Capitoline, Quirinal, Viminal, Esquiline, Coelian,
Aretine, Palatine)

Salesmanship

For the sale :

   Plan aims, etc.

Prepare by research, **l**ose time lose all,
analyse situation, **n**ever just call ;
arrest senses, **i**nterest by questions & novelty
move by proof and demonstration, **s**ucceed in
getting 'yes' ;
evaluate outcome, **t**each yourself and others,
check results.

For the presentation :

   Present

Prepare, **r**ehearse, **e**mphasise main point ;
Showmanship, **e**ncourage participation ;
Notebook (to eliminate digressions) ;
Teaching gets your 'Yeses'.

Sharps and flats, musical

For the order in which sharps are entered in key signature:

Frederick **C**harles **g**oes **d**own **a**nd **e**nds **b**attle.

Reverse order for flats (B, E, A, D, G, C, F)

Simpson's rule

For the area under a curve:

Add first to last, and to this add
Twice even, four times odd.
By one sixth n then multiply,
The area is found, by God!

The formula reads:

$$\text{Area} = \frac{n}{6}[y_0 + y_n + 2(y_2 + y_4 + \ldots) + 4(y_3 + y_5 + \ldots)]$$

Where y = vertical drawn to line of curve from base x, on which n is the common interval.

Sine, cosine, tangent

For the ratios of sides **opposite** (O), **adjacent** (A), and **hypotenuse** (H):

Some **o**fficers **h**ave **c**urly **a**uburn **h**air **t**o **o**ffer **a**ttraction.

The mnemonic represents

$$\text{Sine} = \frac{\text{Opposite side}}{\text{Hypoteneuse}}$$

$$\text{Cosine} = \frac{\text{Adjacent side}}{\text{Hypoteneuse}}$$

$$\text{Tangent} = \frac{\text{Opposite side}}{\text{Adjacent side}}$$

Alternative

Oh **h**eck — **a**nother **h**our **o**f **a**lgebra!

$$\left(\frac{O}{H} = \text{sine}; \frac{A}{H} = \text{cosine}; \frac{O}{A} = \text{tangent} \right)$$

Alternative using different terms

Some **p**eople **h**ave **c**urly **b**rown **h**air **t**hough **p**ainted **b**lack.

This gives
$$\text{Sine} = \frac{\text{Perpendicular}}{\text{Hypoteneuse}}$$

$$\text{Cosine} = \frac{\text{Base}}{\text{Hypoteneuse}}$$

$$\text{Tangent} = \frac{\text{Perpendicular}}{\text{Base}}$$

For the positive functions of sine, cosine, tangent, relative to the angle. Two mnemonics:

All **s**tations **t**o **C**oventry.

Cast.

As in the diagram

$$
\begin{array}{c|c}
S & A \\
\hline
T & C
\end{array}
\quad X
$$

in which each quadrant shows the positive function (A = all).

Measuring angles in an anti-clockwise direction from the point X, **a**ll the trigonometrical functions of angles in the 1st quadrant, the **s**ine function of angles in the 2nd quadrant, the **t**angent function of angles in the 3rd quadrant, and the **c**osine function of angles in the 4th quadrant are positive. All other functions are negative.

Soil

For the chief constituents of soil:

All **h**airy **m**en **w**ill **b**uy **r**azors.

(air, humus, mineral salts, water, bacteria, rock particles)

Spectrum

For the order of colours:

Richard **of** **Y**ork **g**ained **b**attles **in** **v**ain.

(red, orange, yellow, green, blue, indigo, violet)

Alternative

Roll **o**ut **y**our **G**uinness, **b**oys, **in** **v**ats.

Alternative

Real **o**ld **y**okels **g**uzzle **b**eer **in** **v**olume.

Square roots

For the roots of 2, 3 and 5:

I wish I knew
(1·4   1   4)
The root of two.

O charmed was he
(1·7   3   2)
to know the root of three.

So we now strive
(2·2   3   6)
To find root five.

Stars

For the classification of stars in descending order of surface temperature:

Wow! **O**h **b**e **a** **f**ine **g**irl, **k**iss **m**e **r**ight **n**ow **s**weetheart.

(W,O,B,A,F,G,K,M,R,N,S – running from hottest to coolest)

Statistics

For Type I (null = false) and Type II (null = true) errors, when tests of significance are given wrong inferences:

A Type I error is that of an optimist;
A Type II error, that of a pessimist.

('O' comes before 'p').

An optimist tends to see experimental significance, i.e. feels confident he can reject a null hypothesis, before such confidence is warranted. A pessimist tends to do the opposite, i.e. wrongly accept that his experiments fail to show significant results.

Statistics

For the fact that an experimental hypothesis (H_1) is evaluated by testing its logical cover, the null hypothesis (H_0). The probability of an observed result H_0 is expressed as p:

If p is low, reject H_0.

Stave, musical

For placing its notes correctly:

Every **g**ood **b**oy **d**eserves **f**un.

(notes on treble stave lines: e, g, b, d, f)

Face

(notes between treble stave lines: f, a, c, e)

Good **b**oys **d**eserve **f**un **a**lways.

(notes on bass stave lines: g, b, d, f, a)

All **c**ows **e**at **g**rass.

(notes between bass stave lines: a, c, e, g)

Stings, insect

For their treatment:

Use **a**mmonia for a **b**ee sting, **v**inegar for a **w**asp sting.

Mnemonic:
a is followed by **b**, **v** by **w**

Sulphuric acid, dilution

For the safe order of work:

In Remembrance
May her rest be long and placid,
She added water to the acid!
The other girl did what she oughter:
She added acid to the water.

ABCDEFGHIJKLMNOPQR**S**TUVWXYZ

Summertime, British

For gaining/losing the hour:

Forward April
Back September
That is all you need remember.

Alternative

Spring forward, fall back.

Syllogistic moods

For the formulas of a valid mood:

Barbara celarent darii ferio baralipton
Celantes dabitis fapesmo frisesomorum;
Cesare campestres festino baroco; darapti
Felapton disamis datisi bocardo ferison.

This is the best-known of several thirteenth-
century mnemonics for identifying the syllogistic
moods. W. and M. Kneale write of it: 'Each word
is to be taken as the formula of a valid mood and
interpreted according to the following rules: the
first three vowels indicate the quantity and quality
of the three propositions which go to make a
syllogism, **a** standing for the universal affirmative, **e**
for the universal negative, **i** for the particular
affirmative, and **o** for the particular negative; the
initial consonant of each formula after the first four
indicates that the mood is to be reduced to that
mood among the first four which has the same
initial; **s** appearing immediately after a vowel
indicates that the corresponding proposition is to
be converted simply during reduction, while **p** in the
same position indicates that the proposition is to be
converted partially or *per accidens*, and **m** between
the first two vowels of a formula indicates that the
premisses are to be transposed; **c** appearing after one
of the first two vowels indicates that the corresponding
premiss is to be replaced by the negative of the
conclusion for the purpose of a reduction *per
impossibile*. The verses, as given here, have the
defect that the division of lines does not correspond
exactly to the division of figures, and many later
authors have exercised their ingenuity in suggesting
improvements.'

Symbols

For some useful mathematical expressions:

A ' $^{\circ}$ of $\circlearrowright$ sense,	A prime degree of clockwise sense,
$\in$ doubt,	An element of doubt,
$\div \infty$	Divided by infinity
Will help the theorist out.	Will help the theorist out.
So this $\rightarrow$	So this tends to the limit
Which $\Rightarrow$ creation	Which converges to creation
And $\leftrightarrow$ I'm told,	And mutually implies, I'm told,
A transfinite $\sim$.	A transfinite negation.
$A \neq$	A logical diversity
Is $\simeq$	Is asymptotic to
The $\sqrt[4]{}$ of a $\oplus$	The fourth root of a direct sum
(It means the same to you);	(It means the same to you);
So $<$, so $>$,	So 'smaller than', so 'greater than'
$\succ a \, p \mid q$	Contains a joint denial
The $=$	The logical identity
Of Bondi, *Au* and Hoyle.	Of Bondi, Gold and Hoyle.

ABCDEFGHIJKLMNOPQRSTUVWXYZ

Thermocouples

For the direction in which the current flows in a thermocouple made from antimony and bismuth metals:

a b c

(The current flows from the **a**ntimony to the **b**ismuth through the **c**old junction)

Titles

For the order of degree of British hereditary titles:

Did **M**ary **e**ver **v**isit **B**righton **b**each?

(Duke, Marquis, Earl, Viscount, Baron, Baronet)

Toluene, halogenation

For the effect that when chlorine reacts with boiling toluene $C_6H_5CH_3$ in bright sunlight it attacks the side-chain forming $C_6H_5CH_2Cl$, $C_6H_5CHCl_2$ and $C_6H_5CCl_3$, whereas when it reacts with cold toluene in the presence of a catalyst, the nucleus (core) forms ortho- and para-chlorotoluenes.

Cold **c**atalyst **c**ore   (CCC)
Sunlight **s**earches out **s**ide-chain   (SSS)

Treaty of Alliance (1672)

For the names of Charles II's ministers:

Cabal

The word 'cabbala' existed in medieval Latin and indeed was used before 1672 to mean 'the private intrigue of a small body of persons'. However, as a mnemonic today it is used to remember the names of Charles II's ministers who signed the Treaty of Alliance with France against Holland in 1672. Their initials (Clifford, Arlington, Buckingham, Ashley, Lauderdale) make up the word. The word 'cabinet' has no connection with 'cabal', but one could regard these five ministers as the precursor of the institution.

Units

For the multipliers of S.I. Units:

Multiplier	Symbol	Name	Mnemonic
10^{12}	T	tiera	**T**o
10^{9}	G	giga	**g**ive
10^{6}	M	mega	**me**
10^{3}	k	kilo	**k**icks
10^{-3}	m	milli	**m**y
10^{-6}	μ (mu)	micro	**mu**sicians
10^{-9}	n	nano	**n**ow
10^{-12}	p	pico	**p**lay
10^{-15}	f	femto	**f**or
10^{-18}	a	acto	**a**ges.

Vitamins

For the properties of vitamins:

A Food Chemist's Bedtime Story

Vitamin A
Keeps the cold germs away
And tends to make meek people nervy,
B's what you need
When you're going to seed
And C is specific in scurvy.
Vitamin D makes the bones in your knee
Tough and hard for the service on Sunday.
While E makes hens scratch
And increases the hatch
And brings in more profits on Monday.
Vitamin F never bothers the chef
For this vitamin never existed.
G puts the fight in the old appetite
And you eat all the foods that are listed.
So now when you dine remember these lines:
If long on this globe you will tarry
Just try to be good and pick out more food
From the orchard, the garden, and dairy.

ABCDEFGHIJKLMNOPQRSTUV**W**XYZ

Wars of the Roses

For the order of battles between Yorkist and Lancastrian forces:

A **b**oy **n**ow **w**ill **m**ention **a**ll **t**he **h**ot, **h**orrid **b**attles **t**ill **B**osworth.

(St. Albans, Blore Heath, Northampton, Wakefield, Mortimer's Cross, 2nd St. Albans, Towton, Hedgeley Moor, Hexham, Barnet, Tewkesbury, Bosworth)

Zodiac, signs of

For their order:

> Our vernal signs the Ram begins,
> Then comes the Bull, in May the Twins;
> The Crab in June, next Leo shines,
> And Virgo ends the northern signs.
>
> The Balance brings autumnal fruits,
> The Scorpion stings, the Archer shoots;
> December's Goat brings wintry blast,
> Aquarius rain, the Fish comes last.

Alternative

> The Ram, the Bull, the Heavenly Twins,
> And next the Crab, the Lion shines,
> The Virgin and the Scales,
> The Scorpion, Archer and Sea-Goat,
> The Man that bears the watering-pot,
> And Fish with glittering tails.

Subject-index